SILENT REFLECTION

SILENT REFLECTION

REFRESH YOUR MIND BETWEEN NOTIFICATIONS

M S SANDEEP

Anecdote
Publishing House
For the love of quality reading!

Anecdote
Publishing House
For the love of quality reading!

Anecdote Publishing House
2nd Floor 2/15 Lane no. 2 Ansari Road, Daryaganj-110002
Email: info@anecdotepublishinghouse.com
Website: anecdotepublishinghouse.com

Published by Anecdote Publishing House

First Edition 2025
ISBN 978-81-988015-4-8
MRP ₹ 299

Book Promoted and Marketed by Champ Readers Pvt. Ltd.
Cover design by Somesh Kumar Mishra
Layout by Graphic Tailor
Printed by Thomson Press (India) Ltd, New Delhi

72
QUOTES

Acknowledgements

I offer my heartfelt gratitude to my Guru Yogamaya ji, whom I consider as an embodiment of Goddess Saraswathi. Her unwavering light and wisdom have illuminated my darkest hours.

I bow to Hanuman ji, the divine force of strength, courage and devotion, who walks beside me always.

And to every soul who chooses to reflect, grow, and awaken—you are the reason for these pages.

Epigraph

"An idle mind is a Devil's workshop but a creative mind is a fertile playground for God"

–M S Sandeep

THE SELF WITHIN

“

Learn from everyone, yet imitate no one. We must create and walk our own path and one day become a leader ourselves.

WE MUST ALWAYS BE AUTHENTIC TO OURSELVES, IF NOT WE CAN ONLY LOSE EVERYTHING AND GAIN NOTHING BY FOOLING OR BEING DISHONEST WITH OURSELVES.

We must thank all the people who completely give up on us, as this can open the doorway for us to start believing in ourselves.

Even Almighty God cannot save a soul if the soul doesn't have the intent to save itself.

“

We must first transform ourselves before thinking **of and embarking on** changing the world.

LEARNING TO ENJOY OUR OWN COMPANY PAVES THE WAY FOR TRULY ENJOYING THE COMPANY OF OTHERS. IT ALSO GIVES A DEEP SENSE OF SATISFACTION AND JOY WHICH WORDS CANNOT DESCRIBE.

We feel hurt when other people use us for their benefit, yet we don't feel hurt when our own mind has enslaved us since so many decades.

We need to evolve ourselves to such a level such that even if **death** *comes calling the next moment, we can leave happily, without any regrets.*

We must share our positive energy and light with the whole world just like the Sun and not keep it to ourselves.

Meditation is not an activity that we do. Preparation to be in the meditative state is an activity. *Meditation* is a state to be experienced within oneself.

When we are able to look back at our own lives and laugh out loud, then we can look at whole of life in a lighter vein, nothing remains serious, we realize that we were the ones making it appear so serious. Devoid of this seriousness, life is just a drama to be lived and enjoyed, each person has been given a role to play by the creator and it is our duty to fulfill that role to the best of our abilities.

Admitting our mistakes to ourselves first and then to others is a sign of a mature person. A spineless person can never admit their mistakes, either to themselves or to others.

EVERYONE GETS KNOCKED DOWN AT SOME POINT IN LIFE. IT'S HOW WE GET UP AND GET GOING AGAIN THAT DEFINES US.

If we can become our own best friend then we won't have the need to seek out external friends. But when external friends do come into our life, then we can be a true friend to them and give them happiness without expecting anything in return.

We all seem to be in a mad rush to do something, go somewhere or achieve everything instantly. Let's just pause for a moment, take a deep breath, spend time with ourselves and introspect. What is it that we really want in life? Why are we living our life like a machine? Let's come out of the conditioning of society. There's a deeper meaning to life. Let's explore it. Let's wake up from our slumber. We have slept enough already.

A caterpillar can never imagine what it would be like to be a butterfly while in the caterpillar state. It can only experience being a butterfly after going through the difficult and transforming process of Metamorphosis.

"

The truth is One but people perceive the truth in different ways according to their own intelligence and understanding levels, just like in a school where the teacher teaches the same lesson to everyone but the students grasp it according to their own intelligence and understanding levels.

"

MIND, TIME AND STILLNESS

The unreal or delusion or hallucination being projected through the mind as good as reality is what is MAYA.

The worst definition of time is: *'TIME IS MONEY'*.

Overflowing thoughts in the mind put to constructive use is my definition of writing.

Meditation is the process of activating the SIM card of God which is embedded in one's body, mind and soul. Once this SIM is activated, communication with God is possible.

Speaking from the heart (expressing our feelings) rather than speaking from the mind (accusing and blaming others) can prevent a lot of misunderstandings and conflict.

The reason why time goes fast when we are happy but ***moves slowly*** *when we are sad is that, when we are happy, we are less aware of time and when we are sad, we are more aware of time. When our awareness shifts away from time, then we no* ***longer experience time*** *within us, though time is ticking away externally.*

Never believe someone when they say that they don't have the time for us. What they actually mean to say is that we are not their priority.

If we can't have a dream of becoming a king/queen even in our thoughts, then how will we ever become a king/queen in real life?

Over analyzing the past is not good, anticipating and negatively worrying about the future is also not good. The only solution is to be like a witness in the present moment while living and participating in the world, thereby being in a state of timelessness.

PURPOSE, ACTION & GROWTH

Failures can be stepping stones to success but first we must acknowledge that we have failed and also realize the reason/s for failing, otherwise it will just mean repeating the same mistakes again and again without ever tasting success.

IF WE ARE CONVINCED THAT A PARTICULAR HABIT IS GOOD FOR US, THEN WE WILL MOST CERTAINLY CREATE TIME FOR THAT HABIT AND NOTHING CAN STOP US FROM DOING IT.

Beneficial (good) habits can be as addictive as harmful (bad) habits. It's never too late to change.

The least we can do in our lifetime is not to repeat the mistakes of our previous generations and to continue the good work which they had started.

Height of discipline:- When you have the chance to break the rules, yet you choose to follow the rules.

A leader is not someone who wants to grab power or stay in power. A true leader is one who makes others empowered to be leaders themselves.

The major goal of life should be to attain complete mastery over the mind. Once we achieve this, life can become a celebration to enjoy.

LOVE, CONNECTION & HEALING

When we share our happiness and joy with others it not only makes others happy but it also multiplies the happiness within us. So, let's be happy, make everyone around us happy and make the world a better place to live in.

A doctor once grimly told her patient that she has maximum 2 years left to live. The patient was overjoyed and thanked the doctor. The doctor was astonished and asked her why she was so happy. The patient replied that she had been ‘dead’ all these years and now she has a reason to live life to the fullest.

WHEN WE ARE SEEKING TRUE LOVE, THEN LOVE HAS MYSTERIOUS AND MAGICAL WAYS OF FINDING US.

We should think **100 TIMES** before stepping on a caterpillar, as we would indirectly be killing a **BUTTERFLY.**

When we realize that every individual is doing the best they can in the given circumstances and that their actions are based on their level of awareness at any given point of time, then it's easy to forgive those who have hurt us or treated us badly.

Physical pain by its nature peaks immediately after an injury and subsides over time. Emotional pain however is like a wave. It keeps resurfacing at regular intervals based on triggers.

SPIRITUAL WISDOM

We are all players in a Cosmic Multi-billion player Real-time Game of Life created by God. The Goal is to progress from one level to the next higher level until we reach the ultimate God level.

We must always be 100 % truthful to our Doctor, our Lawyer and the silent witness residing within us called Sakshi, God or Almighty creator.

God doesn't require humans to praise him/ her or worship him/her, but people who have realized the presence of God within them can't help but praise and worship God.

When we handover the keys of our life to God, then life truly becomes beautiful.

Life becomes a lot simpler if we realize that we are just actors in the Cosmic drama of life. Situations are created by the Director (God). Our role is to give our best performance in all the scenes.

SPIRITUALITY AND RELIGION ARE NEITHER OPPOSITES NOR ARE THEY MUTUALLY EXCLUSIVE. A SPIRITUAL PERSON CAN BE RELIGIOUS AND A RELIGIOUS PERSON CAN ALSO BE SPIRITUAL.

EVERY HUMAN BEING HAS THE POTENTIAL TO AWAKEN THE DIVINITY WITHIN THEM, REALIZE THEIR HIGHEST POTENTIAL AND LITERALLY BECOME GOD-LIKE THEMSELVES, IF THEY MAKE THE SINCERE EFFORT.

Spirituality can bring out the lion in us whereas religion only serves to turn us into a sheep.

LIFE TRANSFORMING INSIGHTS

A *BEAUTIFUL* painting is lifeless and has no meaning if there is no observer left to appreciate its *BEAUTY*.

However fast we travel on the road, there will always be someone ahead of us, simply because they have started earlier than us.

A firefighter uses water to extinguish even the most intense fires, then why do we use 'fire' to fight 'fire' at home, office and in life in general?

Life is not a rat race or cat race or dog race, it is a journey of a human being to be experienced and lived from start to finish.

Some people get more respect than they deserve because of the Chair they are sitting in. If we don't stand up to such people who misuse their power and authority, then we have ourselves to blame.

IF YOU LIVE WITH THE QUESTIONS LONG ENOUGH, THEN YOU WILL CERTAINLY GET THE ANSWERS.

In order to overcome emotional pain, one must first acknowledge the pain, feel it completely, heal and then move on.

For World peace to be achieved, the “Bad” needs to end and the “Good” needs to prevail. Both Bad and Good exist within each individual. Hence each individual needs to conquer the ‘Bad’ in them and make the ‘Good’ prevail.

What matters more is not how many people come to attend our funeral, but how many people are there for us by our side at the moments in our life when we 'die' while still being alive.

Inspiration truly stands for something that is gained by observing and absorbing the good in each individual whom we come across in life. It's next to impossible to go wrong when we have this attitude.

WE MUST BE WITH SOMEONE WHO BRINGS OUT THE BEST QUALITIES IN US, NOT THE WORST IN US.

The first step towards becoming a legend is to stop blindly following the crowd.

The World will go on even without us. But we have the choice and power to make the world a better place while we are still alive.

The more we get to know ourselves, the more we get to know others as well, because all human beings are connected.

When we realize that death can strike any moment of any day, then we will focus only on those things that really matter to us and thereby lead a fulfilling life.

Acceptance and patience are two of the greatest qualities that a human being can possess. It can save a person from a lot of suffering.

The people who are by our side and have faith in us, when we are a "**Nobody**", truly deserve to be with us when we become a "**Somebody**".

A contribution of Five hundred from an amount of fifty thousand has more worth and value than a contribution of Five hundred from an amount of **Five lakhs**.

Our destination lies 100 km to the north but we keep travelling 100s of km in the south direction, then how can we ever expect to reach our destination?

If we have the courage to take the road not taken, then we give a chance for life to pleasantly surprise and reward us.

Life is all about priorities. What we give priority to grows in our life. If we make happiness a priority of our life, then we will experience more happiness in our life on a daily basis. Hence, we must choose our priorities wisely.

When the going gets tough, the tough seek help to get going again.

PLAYFUL WISDOM

When life gives us lemons, let's not just make lemon juice and drink it, but plant the seeds of the lemon to grow a lemon tree which will give us enough lemons to make lemon juice for the rest of our life.

Life is similar to the stock market. We all have high (bullish) days, low (bearish) days and neutral (flat) days.

Devoid of sound, a horror movie is reduced to a comedy movie.